LEARN TO LANDSCAPE

Master Realistic Color Garden Guide Of Concept, Tools And Technique To Landscape And Garden

INTRODUCTION

Writing down a plan is the most crucial step in designing a landscape for a house. You can save money and time by creating a master plan, which also increases the likelihood that your design will be successful. A master plan is created through a process known as "design." It is a systematic approach that considers your surroundings, preferences, design concepts, and features. The objective is to arrange your yard's natural and artificial components into an attractive, functional, and environmentally friendly landscape.

Landscaping makes a house or other exciting things on a piece of land look better. It is done so that grass, trees, and bushes can be planted to make a natural scene. Landscape gardening is both an art and a science that involves setting up a plot of land to look like a natural landscape. It can also be thought of as making a garden look like nature. It can also be thought of as improving people's living environment. The way a landscape looks can be happy, bold, quiet, calm, etc. This phrase will be suitable for the place and the reason. It shouldn't be a group of exciting things but a picture.

The landscape is so beautiful that it shows the feeling or mood of the landscape, such as excitement, sadness, seriousness, or awe. There are many things about a beautiful landscape that can make life feel better. Since landscape gardening is about making pictures with plants and other items on the ground, a landscape designer should know about art, ornamental gardening, ecology, and physiology. He should be an architect or engineer to understand how shapes, colors, and buildings are related.

PRINCIPLES OF LANDSCAPING

Since it is influenced by things like plant growth, the weather, and how people utilize space, the "art" is constantly changing. As a result, to ensure that the design looks nice, operates well, and is beneficial for the environment, landscape designers utilize a design process that considers all aspects of the environment, the land, the growing plants, and the user's demands. This ensures that the design is visually beautiful and advantageous to the environment.

Elements of landscaping

The landscape design process starts with figuring out what the user needs and wants and what the site is like. Using this information, the designer then puts together the features, which are the plants and hardscape materials. The elements of a pleasing design, such as color, line, shape, texture, and visual weight, can describe how the features look. The principles are the basic ideas of composition, such as proportion, order, repetition, and unity. They tell you how to set up or organize the features to make a landscape that looks good.

To design a landscape and move through the design process, you must understand the elements and principles of design. This book discusses each aspect, the regulations, and how to use them.

Elements of design

Composition elements are the things that people see and react to when they look at a space. People can feel many different things based on what they see, and the more positive those feelings are, the more likely they will enjoy and use a space. The line is one of the most common parts of a piece of writing. The line can help in many ways to make landscape shapes and patterns.

Line

Lines in the landscape can be made by the edge between two materials, the outline or silhouette of a shape, or a long, straight feature. Lines are a powerful tool for a designer because they can make any shape or form and control eye and body movements. Landscape designers use lines to make patterns, shape spaces, create shapes, control movement, show who is in charge, and give a landscape a consistent theme. Landscape lines can be made in a few ways: when two different materials meet on the ground plane, like where the edge of a brick patio meets a large area of green grass; when the advantages of an object are visible or stand out against a background, like when the outline of a tree stands out against the sky; or when a material is placed in a line, like a fence. Figure 1 shows bedlinens, hardscape lines, path lines, sod lines, fence lines, and sod lines. Lines might have one or more qualities, but they are usually used for different things.

Properties of lines

People's emotional and physical responses to the landscape depend on how lines are made.

Straight lines

Straight lines are solid. They give a design a formal look, are usually part of a symmetrical design, and lead the eye straight to a focal point. Diagonal lines are just straight lines that go in a certain way. Most hardscape edges and materials have straight lines.

Curved lines

Curved lines give things a casual, natural, and easygoing feel that is more associated with the outdoors and asymmetry. Curved lines move the eye more slowly and create hidden views that add mystery to the space. Plants like trees or tall structures like a birdhouse on a pole or an arbor

Horizontal lines

Horizontal lines are essential as they move the eye along the ground plane and make a space feel bigger. Low bars are more subdued and make you feel like you can relax. Horizontal lines can be used to divide or connect areas. Low garden walls, paths, and short hedges make for soft lines.

On a plan, shapes are drawn with lines. They show where plant beds and hardscape areas are in plan view. The vertical forms also make lines of things like buildings and plants. Bedlinen, hardscape lines, and plant lines are the three main lines that shape a landscape. Bedlinen is made where the edge of the plant bed meets another surface material, like grass, groundcover, gravel, or patio pavers. Bedlinen connects plants to the house and hardscape because the eye follows the line, which moves the gaze through the landscape. The edge of the hardscape, which marks the built structure, makes the hardscape lines. Lines, like a fence or wall, can also be made with long, thin things.

Vertical lines

Lines that go up and down move the eye and make a space feel bigger. An upward line can draw attention to a feature and gives the impression of movement. Vertical lines in the landscape can be made with tall, thin forms.

The shape is an outline that fills a space, and form is the mass of that shape in three dimensions. The form can be found in both hardscapes and plants. It is usually the most noticeable thing in a landscape, and it often determines the style of a garden. The shape of structures, plant beds, and garden decorations also affects the garden's overall shape. Circles, squares, and polygons are all examples of formal geometric shapes. Simple and naturalistic forms have wavy lines, organic edges, and broken edges. The outlines or silhouettes form in a garden of plants, but the space between plants can also form.

Geometric forms

Form in a circle

Circles can be whole circles or cut into half circles or circle segments and put together with lines to make arcs and tangents. Figure 2 shows how circle segments can be used to make panels for hardscapes and lawns. For more variety and interest, circles can also be stretched into ovals and ellipses. The eye is always attracted to the center of a circle, which can be used to draw attention to a focal point or connect other shapes.

Square form

Squares are easy to work with when building, so they are often used for stepping stones, bricks, tiles, and wooden structures. The square shape can also be broken up into smaller pieces and used over and over to make a grid pattern. Squares differ from circles in that their edges are more robust and can be lined up or overlapped to create unique designs and more complex shapes.

Irregular polygons

Polygons are shapes with many straight sides. For example, a triangle is a three sides polygon with three sides. Polygons with angled edges can make interesting shapes, but they should be used carefully because they can get complicated. It's best to keep things simple.

Meandering lines

Meandering lines often look like the way rivers or streams flow naturally. They are smooth lines with deep curves that go up and down. Figure 3 shows that meandering lines work well for paths, plant beds, and dry stream beds. By leading people around corners to find new views and spaces, meandering lines can add mystery and interest to a garden.

Organic edges

Organic edges look like the edges of natural things like leaves, plant shapes, and rocks. They are rough and uneven. You can find organic lines in rock gardens and along dry creek beds or make them on the edges of hardscapes.

Fragmented edges

Fragmented edges look like broken stones or pavers strewn along the border. They are often used to make a gradual edge on patios or walkways.

Plant forms

The thing that lasts the longest about a plant is its shape. The form is the most consistent and easy-to-recognize trait of plants, so common plant forms are well-known and standardized. The condition can also be made by grouping plants together. A group of plants has a different shape than a single plant. A strong form that stands out from the rest of the piece will be given more attention within the article. Care must be taken when using a form with much contrast. One or two work perfectly as a focal point, but too many cause chaos. The bulk of the composition should be made up of natural plant forms, not over-trimmed ones. The importance of overall shape depends on how you look at it. For example, the shape of a tree can look very different when standing under its canopy and far away in an open field. Forms that go up add height, while forms that go across add width. Plant shapes also make and define empty spaces or voids between the plants. These voids can have either

convex or concave shapes. High-arching tree branches usually make an open space under the hollow tree, while a round canopy supported with low branches fills the area to make it convex.

Tree-shapes

Most trees are round, columnar, oval, pyramidal, vase-shaped, or weeping (figure 6). Different tree shapes are used to make them look nice, but they are also crucial for their work. A round or oval tree is suitable for creating a shady area in the garden, while a columnar or pyramidal tree is better for making a screen. A weeping tree makes an excellent focal point.

Shrub forms

There are many different shapes of shrubs, such as upright, vase-shaped, arching, mounding, rounded, spiky, cascading, and irregular. Often, the form of a shrub depends on whether it will be used in a group or as a single plant. Shrubs that mound or spread out look best in a group, while shrubs that cascade or have a vase shape look like single plants.

Groundcover forms

Groundcovers can be mat-like, spread out, cluster together, sprawl out, or have short spikes. Almost all groundcovers look better when there are a lot of them because they are usually small, ground-hugging plants that don't stand out much on their own.

Properties of form

People can often recognize and name a feature based on its outline or silhouette. This makes the form very powerful. People can often see a shape even when they can only see part. The eye fills in the rest based on what it knows and what it thinks it sees. Patterns, the primary way the landscape is put together, can only be made by repeating shapes.

The form is also the main thing that makes a garden formal or informal. Formal gardens that follow an established style, like contemporary or Italian gardens, often have geometric shapes with straight lines. Forms in a peaceful garden are more natural and organic, like those in gardens that try to look like nature. Form compatibility is another important part of design unity. Having one or two very different forms is suitable for contrast and highlighting, but most other forms should have some similarities for a unified look.

Texture

The texture is a way to describe how rough or smooth the surface of a plant or hardscape material feels or looks. The texture makes things different, engaging, and stand out. The plant has different textures in its leaves, flowers, bark, and overall branching pattern. The surface of a plant is often based on the size and shape of its leaves. Most of the time, you can say that a plant has a coarse, medium, or fine texture. The rough surface is more important than the texture, which is fine. It also tends to be more critical in terms of color and shape. The fine texture is less important and tends to bring a composition together. Plants with a rough surface tend to draw the eye and keep it there because the light and dark shadows add more interest. The fine texture makes distances seem more significant and gives the impression of more open space. RA's rough surface makes plants look closer together and makes the area feel smaller or enclosed. Texture can also be found in the hardscape, such as on buildings, patios, walls, and walkways.

Coarse texture

Some of the things about a plant that gives it a coarse texture are its large leaves, its leaves with very irregular edges, its bold, deep veins, its colors that change, its thick twigs and branches, its leaves and twigs with spines or thorns, and its bold, thick, and irregular shapes. A plant with a rough texture has a looser form because each leaf breaks up the outline. Philodendrons, agaves, bromeliads, hollies, palms, and hydrangeas are all plants with a rough texture. Hardscapes with a coarse texture include rough-cut stone, rough-finished brick, unfinished wood with knots, and a raised grain. The material used for building for a long time and still has a rough surface is often coarse.

Fine texture

Small leaves, thin, strappy leaves (on grasses) or tall, slender stems, tiny, dense twigs and branches, long stems (on vines), and small, delicate flowers are all signs of fine texture. People often say they are light and wispy or look like a sprawling vine. Some plants with a fine texture, like boxwoods, have a more robust shape because the small leaves are close together, making a solid edge. Grass, ferns, Japanese maples, many vines, and junipers with fine needles all have a fine texture. Smooth stone, wooden or ceramic pots, and glass ornaments are all examples of hardscapes with a fine texture. Fine-textured water is soft, like the water in a reflecting pool, or has a fine spray.

Medium grain

Most plants don't have a coarse or fine texture. Instead, they have a surface that is somewhere in between. They have leaves about the size of a hand and have simple shapes and smooth edges. The average-sized branches are neither close together nor far apart, and the shape of the tree as a whole is usually round or mound-like. Plants with a medium texture are used as a background to connect and tie together plants with a coarse and delicate texture. Agapanthus, Ardisia, camellia, euonymus, pittosporum, and viburnum are all plants with a medium texture. Medium-textured hardscapes include standard flagstone pavers, broom-brushed concrete, and finished woods.

Properties of texture

Your perception of distance and size shifts depending on the textures you look at. Arrange the plants in your garden so that the ones with the finest surfaces are on the outer, the ones with medium textures are in the middle, and the plants with the coarsest textures are closest to the observer. This will make the space feel bigger. Because the fine texture is slight, it blends into the background and makes things seem farther away. Place coarse textures around the edges of a room and delicate surfaces close to the viewer to make the room feel smaller. The rough texture gives the plants a closer look and makes the room feel smaller. How plants feel can also change depending on how close you are to them. From far away, plants that look rough up close can look smooth. Bold colors make the texture stand out more and make it look rougher, while muted colors can make the surface look smoother. Hardscape with a coarse texture, like very rough rocks and big, bold timbers, tends to make all plant material look like it has a medium texture. Designers will often make a texture study (figure 8) on paper to help them figure out how to put plant materials together. The drawing uses different line weights and distances between lines to show fine, medium, and coarse textures.

Color

Color in plants and hardscapes makes the landscape more interesting and gives it more variety. Color is the most prominent part of a landscape, and most homeowners focus on it. However, it is also the most temporary part since most plants only bloom for a few weeks a year. Color schemes are put together with the help of color theory and the color wheel. Red, blue, and yellow are the three primary colors. Green, orange, and violet are the three secondary colors made by mixing two primary colors. The six tertiary colors, like red-orange, are made by mixing two adjacent primary and secondary colors. The color theory studies how colors work together and how they should be used in art. There are three basic color schemes: monochromatic, similar, and different.

Monochromatic scheme

A color scheme with only one color is called monochromatic. In landscaping, this usually means that the leaves are another color besides green. An utterly green garden depends more on its shape and texture for contrast and interest. One color can come in light and dark shades, making it more interesting. A white garden with white flowers, white leaves with different shades of white, and white garden decor is an example of a monochromatic scheme.

Analogous scheme

Analogous (sometimes called "harmonious") color schemes use three to five colors next to themselves on the color wheel, red-orange, like red, orange, yellow-orange, and yellow, or blue, blue-violet, and violet. The colors are related because they are usually made by mixing two primary colors to make secondary and two tertiary colors. This means that they have similar qualities.

A system that works together

On the color wheel, colors opposite each other are said to be complementary. They are typically highly dissimilar to one another in many respects. The color combinations most frequently seen are violet and yellow, red and green, blue and orange, and green and red. Flowers typically have two hues that complement one another effectively. There is much connectivity between these two colors.

Plant and hardscape color

Plants have color in their petals, leaves, bark, and fruit. Most of the time, the background color for flower colors comes from foliage. By number, green leaves in all their different shades are the most common color, but other colors stand out more because they are so different from green. Buildings, rocks, pavers, wood, and furniture all have color. Most of the colors in the stone, wood, and other natural materials, like brown, tan, and pale yellow, are muted. The majority of the vibrant colors in the hardscape are from man-made objects, such as painted furniture, vividly colored ceramic containers or sculptures, and glass ornaments.

Properties of color

Color is an essential part of making the landscape exciting and different. Colors have qualities that can change how we feel, how we see space, how the light looks, how we balance things, and how we put things in focus. One way to talk about a color's quality is temperature. Colors can seem cool or warm, affecting how you feel. Cool colors tend to be soothing, so they should be used where you want to relax and feel calm. Warm colors are more exciting and should be used in places where people gather, like parties and gatherings. The "temperature" of colors can also change how far away they look. Cool colors tend to move back and make things seem farther away. This creates a room that feels more enormous. Warm colors tend to move forward and make things seem closer, which makes a room feel smaller.

Color can also draw people's attention and show them where to look. Bright colors can be used to make focal points. For example, bright yellow has the most intense and stands out against all other colors. This is often called a "pop" of color, and you should use it sparingly. When it comes to how it looks, a small amount of solid color is just as substantial as a large amount of a weaker color. Different colors can be used in the garden at other times. Summer colors are brighter and more varied, with more flowers, while winter colors are darker and more uniform, with more leaves. Color is also affected by the quality of the light, which changes throughout the day and year. In the summer, when the sun is brighter and more substantial, colors look more saturated and bright, while in the winter, when the light is more muted, colors look more muted. When picking a color scheme, you should think about what time of day you will use the yard. Color changes should draw attention to things that will last longer, like texture and shape. A plan view of a color study (figure 9) can help you choose colors. On the plan, color schemes are drawn to show how much each color will be used and where it will be.

Visual weight

Visual weight is the idea that certain combinations of mass and contrast make certain composition parts more critical. Some features of a piece stand out and are easy to remember, while others blend into the background. This d means that the things in the environment are o. optional They tie together things with much visual weight and give the eye a place to rest. When all the parts have much visual weight, the eye tends to jump from one piece to the next, making the whole thing look messy. High visible weight usually comes from a group of plants with one or more traits: upright or unusual shapes, large size, bright colors, bold textures, and diagonal lines. Low visual weight comprises thin horizontal lines, flat or soft conditions, delicate texture, and muted or dull colors.

Principles of design

Landscape designers use design principles to organize elements in a good way. Using the rules of proportion, order, repetition, and unity, you can make a piece that sounds good together. All the controls are connected, and the following helps you reach the other rules. Comfort, both physically and mentally, is an integral part of the design, and these principles can help you get there. People feel more at ease when there is order and repetition in the environment. Landscapes that are well-kept and have predictable patterns (which are signs of human care) are easier to "read" and tend to put people at ease. Psychological comfort is also affected by how happy a person feels when they look at a landscape that fits together nicely. Users are more physically comfortable, can do their jobs better, and feel safer in a landscape the same size as a person.

Proportion

Relative proportion is how big something is in comparison to other things. Total balance is how big or small something is. The size of the human body is an essential absolute scale in design because the size of the human body measures everything else. Plants, garden structures, and decorations should all be sized for people. The size of the house, the yard, and the area to be planted are also significant relative sizes.

Proportion in plants

Plants can show proportion by growing around people, other plants, and the house. The piece feels balanced and tuned when all three are in the right amounts. Having the same open space and space with plants can also give a sense of balance. Using different-sized plants can help you emphasize a large plant by making it stand out. Using plants of the same size over and over, you can create a sense of rhythm.

Proportion in hardscape

People find features most valuable when they fit their bodies. Benches, tables, paths, arbors, and gazebos work best when they are easy to use and make people feel at ease. The hardscape should also be in scale with the house. For example, a deck or patio should be big enough to hold parties but not so big that it overwhelms the house.

Proportions in voids

For comfort in voids or open spaces, human scale is also essential. Patios and terraces are small hollow spaces that make people feel safer. The enclosure is an integral part of wellness in the 'area. Most people feel safe when something is above them, like a ceiling. The section can be something other than solid. An implied enclosure, like tree branches, works well as a psychological enclosure that still lets in light and lets you see the sky.

Order

Order usually means how the space is laid out or how the design is put together, and it is generally achieved through balance. Balance is the idea that something has the same weight and visual appeal around a real or imagined central axis. Balance is affected by shape, color, size, and feel. Balance can be symmetrical, asymmetrical, or from a different point of view. You can also create order by grouping other parts or features and putting them around a central point.

Symmetrical balance

This is called symmetrical balance when the same things (mirror images) are on both sides of an axis. This balance is used in traditional designs and is one of the oldest and most sought-after ways to arrange space. This is because the human mind naturally divides space by imagining a central axis and then tries to spread objects or mass out evenly (visual weight). This idea is used to set up a lot of old gardens.

Asymmetrical balance

Asymmetrical balance is reached when different shapes, colors, or textures on either side of an axis have the same weight to the eye. This kind of balance is not formal, and it is usually created by groups of plants that look the same in terms of their visual weight rather than their total weight. Plants, structures, and garden decorations can be used together to make the mass. To create balance, things with big sizes, familiar shapes, bright colors, and rough textures look heavier and should be used sparingly; in co-contrast, stuff with small dimensions, loose bodies, gray or muted colors, and delicate textures look lighter and should be used more. Perspective balance

Perspective balance involves how the foreground, middle ground, and background look together. When you look at composition, the things in the front are usually more important because they are closer to you. You can balance this by making the background brighter or rougher. Most of the time, the focus should be on the foreground or the ground.

Many collections

The mass collection is the process of grouping things based on their similarities and then putting them around a central space or something. A good example is putting plants in a circle around an open lawn or gravel seating area.

Repetition

This is called repetition when elements or features are used repeatedly to make patterns or a sequence in the landscape. The rhythm of the landscape is made up of lines, shapes, colors, and textures that repeat. Repetition should be used carefully because too much of it can be tedious, and too little of it can be unclear. Simple repetition is when the same thing is used in a line or when geometric shapes, like squares, are put together in an organized pattern.

Alternation, a slight change in the regular order of things, can make repetition more interesting. For example, every fifth square in a line could be a circle. Inversion is a type of alternation in which some elements are changed so that their traits are the opposite of what they were before. For example, you could have a row of plants in the shape of vases and a row of plants in the form of pyramids.

Gradation, when some parts of a feature change slowly over time, is another way to make something repeated more interesting. For example, you could use a square shape that gets bigger or smaller over time. Patterns aren't always caused by repetition; sometimes, it's just repeatedly using the same color, texture, or shape in the landscape.

Repetition in plants and hardscape

When designing a landscape, repetition refers to employing the same plant in multiple locations. In a grass garden, you may notice some subtle recurrence of the plants. Gradation can be achieved by gradually increasing or decreasing size or height (e.g., using little grasses to create a befitting design from the front, backed by medium grasses and then large grasses). Plants that change from fine to coarse texture or light green to dark green show this more clearly.

Material can be used repeatedly in a yard to make it look cohesive, but it can be made more interesting by changing its color, size, or texture in small ways. The hardscape is the best place to show repetition and pattern because it is easy to copy built materials made to exact dimensions.

Unity

Unity is created by tying together parts and elements to give the whole thing a consistent feel of agreement cement, sometimes called harmony, which means that everything works well together. On the other hand, disorganized groups of plants and garden decorations that don't go together are the opposite of unity. When you arrange colors, textures, and forms, you can create harmony by using dominance, interconnecting three agreements (I'll explain below), and simplicity. Hardscapes and plants can look good together if they have similar features, but it's also essential to have some differences to keep things interesting. The easiest way to bring everything together is to use a design theme or style. Design styles and articles have a clear set of characteristics that have kept them famous because they look good to many people.

Unity by dominance

A plant or object has dominance or emphasis if it draws and keeps people's attention, making it an essential part of the plant or object. The difference between an object and its surroundings usually makes it stand out. A brightly colored ceramic pot next to green plants would be an excellent example in a garden.

Focal points are the things that draw the most attention. Focal points draw attention to a particular spot, move the eye around the space, or help people get where they need to go. Differences in size, color, shape, or texture make things stand out.

People often call plants that stand out "specimen plants." these plants stand out from the others because of their shape, size, or texture. Ordinary plants can also draw attention to something by putting them in a pot (figure 15) or open space. Putting plants in this way is meant to draw attention to the plant. Usually, specimen plants are used to draw attention to doors, paths, or statues. Garden decorations are also good at getting people's attention because they are often very different from plants. Most of the time, plants' shapes and colors are other things. The conditions of sculptures, planters, and furniture are easy to tell apart from the bodies of plants.

Unity by linking together

The concept of connectivity is present in every design and denotes that many components physically interact. Even while every feature has some connection to every other part, the goal should be to make those connections invisible so that the features read as a coherent whole. Because it is so frequently utilized to organize and link together different sections of a landscape, hardscape is an essential component of connectivity. Continuity of a line, like a path, the edge of a building, or a clearly defined edge of a plant bed, can bring everything together by linking it.

Three as one

When things are put together in groups of three or other odd numbers, like five or seven, they look more balanced and give a stronger sense of unity. When you have an odd number, you can have different heights, like small, medium, and large, which make things more interesting. Odd numbers are often seen as a group and are more challenging to separate visually than even numbers.

Unity by simplicity

Simplicity is the idea of taking away or reducing things that aren't necessary to avoid a cluttered look. This makes the design clear and gives it a purpose. Many designers achieve simplicity by carefully removing parts of a structure without its overall shape.

Applying the principles and elements of design

Even though it's helpful to understand the elements and principles of design, it can take time to decide how to use them in your plans for your yard. Each site has challenges and opportunities for innovation and expression, and it needs to use the elements and principles in its way. A good start is to look at a design you like and see how the details and regulations have been used. The best way to develop a good plan is to take ideas from designs you want and change them to fit your site's needs.

Style of person and sense of place

Think about other yards or landscapes you like to figure out what your style is. Look around your neighborhood and the different areas in your town. Look at the ones you want and write down what they have and what plant material they use. Try to figure out the design elements, like color, texture, and shape, and how the line is used in the landscape. Look at the view and figure out how it has balance and rhythm. Also, determine who is in charge and how unity is made. Learning about your neighborhood and community landscapes is essential because most people feel better when they "fit in" with their neighbors. People often have a solid social need to feel like they are a part of the community and make a positive difference in their neighborhood. Having a sense of place, or "genus loci," is the idea that you belong where you are. Sense of place also refers to the area's natural and planned landscapes, which affect the plant and design materials used.

Demonstrations of local botanical gardens, gardens or landscapes, and displays at local nurseries are good places to get ideas. Avoid the big national chain stores' nurseries because their plants are only sometimes grown locally, and their selection might be better for your area. They are, however, an excellent way to buy short-term annuals for small spaces. Go to demonstration gardens and botanical gardens to find groups of plants that are interesting and appealing. Take note of each group's microclimate to see if it will work in your yard.

Because these gardens are made for your area, you can use the same mix of plants as long as they get the right amount of sun and shade. Find out how to grow and take care of the plants to see if they will work for you. You can get several plants in pots and put them together at local nurseries to see how they look. Even though they are small, you can still learn much about texture and color composition from them.

Searching for inspiration in books and publications is yet another method for determining your style. Take notes based on what you see in the photographs as you look at them. How do you like the way it looks? Will it work where you want it to? You won't be able to copy the exact design because your site will be in a different place, be a different size, and have a different shape. However, there are often many parts of the design that you can use on your site. You can replace the hardscape materials and plants in the sample design with ones that are right for your area by choosing materials and plants with the same traits. Think about what the features will look like in your yard and where you might put them. A final design can be made by putting together several different ideas. Remember that the yards and gardens you see in magazines and books were chosen because they are great examples. Most of the time, these gardens are cared for by people who know much about gardening. Think about your maintenance skills and knowledge, or those of your contractor, and change the design as needed.

Terms and conditions

How can you tell if a design you like will work in your yard? First, compare the houses' styles and look for things that your home and the sample house have in common. Look at the sample design's hardscape materials. Does your place look good with the same colors and materials? What could you use instead and still get the look you want if you had to? Imagine the same or similar plant materials around your house. Keep in mind that the plants can be arranged in different ways to fit the size of your yard. For more on choosing plants, see the right plant, right place: the art and science of landscape design: picking the right plants and where to put them.

Second, compare the shape and size of your house's footprint to the shape and size of your lot. For this, you will need an official survey of the property's boundaries that shows the exact impression, including its size and where it is on the property. This will let you know if you have enough space for the features you want and where you can put them. Pay close attention to how the spaces between your house and the property lines are shaped. These are the part where your features will be, and they will help you figure out what those features might look like. For example, a yard that is square may look best with hardscape shapes that are also square. The form of your house will also help you figure out what shape to use in your yard. If the house's walls are in a hexagon or a diagonal, this could lead to a hexagon or diagonal shape in the yard. On the plan, designers often draw lines from the edges or corners of the house to the property lines.

Third, know your site and how you want to use it inside and out. Start by taking stock of and analyzing the site. Make a list of everything about the space and consider how it might affect your design. Each condition can be seen as either an opportunity, which is a good thing that will help you reach your design goal, or a constraint, which is a bad thing that might affect your design but could be turned into an opportunity. Landforms like slopes and flat areas, natural features like trees and rocks, and built features like swimming pools and fences are all examples of options and/or limitations. Depending on the design you want to make, each could be a chance or a problem.

Locating features and defining outdoor rooms

Once you know the architectural style, the shape of the yard spaces, and the possibilities of your site, you can start to place and shape the features. Most features will have a place that makes sense based on how they are used or what they are and what the site offers. Most people think of the yard as an extension of the house, so it makes sense to put the most used parts of the yard near the back door. For example, the patio or deck where you eat or sit outside is usually next to the house for convenience and comfort. Other features, like dog runs and vegetable gardens, are often put on the side of the house to hide them from view. Play or recreation areas often fully view the kitchen or family room, so parents can enjoy seeing their children while playing.

Creating outdoor rooms means dividing a yard into different areas for different uses. This is one of the best ideas in outdoor design. The "rooms" are put together to make the landscape work and look good. Spaces can be defined by using different materials, like the edge of a stone patio against a lawn panel, an elevation change (steps), a form, like a square lawn panel, or a feature, like a low garden wall or small trees, or plants to create the illusion of walls and ceilings. W The elements and principles of design are beneficial when making a room because they help add interest, define spaces and create a unified, functional, and aesthetically pleasing landscape.

Texture and color can also make spaces stand out by giving each one a different look. Using visual weight is another way to show the order of spaces or rooms. High-priority areas can have features and elements that give them much visual weight and draw attention to them. Scale and proportion are good ways to organize and rank things in space. When compared to the other areas, a space that is a very different size tends to be seen as more important. Scale also plays a significant role in deciding what features can be used in a landscape. Other uses need different amounts of space to work. For example, swimming pools, dog runs, and vegetable gardens all have minimum sizes that must be met. A patio's minimum size depends on how many people will use it simultaneously.

Spaces can be linked by lines, like pathways, or they can be linked visually by using emphasis (focal points) that draw attention and lead the eye or by repeating elements that link spaces with similar things. Direction, or how people move through an area, is another essential part of outdoor design. Movement or circulation can be controlled by using different materials, setting up the space, making focal points, and marking paths on purpose. Using all the principles will ensure that the whole landscape looks and works well. Landscape design is all about solving problems by using horticultural science, artful composition, and spatial planning to make attractive and functional outdoor "rooms" that can be used for different things. Line, shape, texture, color, and visual weight are elements, and proportion, order, repetition, and unity of design are principles. These make spaces, connect them, and look good to the eye.

PLANNING YOUR PROJECT

Before you start planting, there are some essential things to consider, whether you want to change your landscape or make a few changes. Many people go to their local gardening store to look at the plants, but if you make a plan, you can choose plants that will meet your needs and do well in your yard.

It's easy to be tempted by beautiful plants at the garden store and buy them, only to find out when you get them home that they won't work in your yard. These tips will help you make a plan and get you on the way to making a landscape that is beautiful, well-kept, and full of life.

1. Know your yard

When planning your landscape, think about the weather in your area, the shape of your land, and the type of soil you have. A good begin this stage to start is with the USDA Plant Hardiness Zone Map. Remember that your yard will likely have its microclimate because of its length and time in the sun and shade.

Most microclimates fall into one of four groups: full sun, partial shade, shade, or deep shade. When choosing plants for your landscape, keep your microclimate in mind. As you plan, you should also consider how the land around your site slopes and how water flows through your landscape. The best landscaping will move moisture away from your house and into other yard parts.

2. Who is going to use your yard?

Think about who will use your yard and how they will use it. Will kids use your yard? Have you got any pets? Do you want to use your yard to have parties outside? Remember that plantings and hardscapes can be used differently to create different landscape spaces. Walkways allow people to move about from one location to another.

Because you intend to use and maintain your yard (or pay someone else to do it), you should consider how you would like to preserve it and the amount of money you have available to invest toward the task. This is because you intend to use and maintain your yard. Make an effort to be as truthful as possible to the best of your abilities. How much time will it take to plan, build, and maintain your outdoor space after it is finished? Or, if you don't think you'll have the time to do it yourself, do you think you'll have the money to pay someone else to do it for you if you don't think you'll have the time to do it yourself? How much of an economic commitment do you anticipate making to cultivate your garden? If you give the answers to these questions some critical consideration, you can help ensure that your landscape will continue to look lovely for many years.

3. Consider themes

Having a theme in mind when designing your landscape will help you select the appropriate materials and plants to use. Pieces can be as straightforward as using the same shapes or forms throughout your yard, creating a relaxation or oriental garden. Either way, they can be broken down into a variety of subthemes.

The style of your home's architecture is an excellent location to begin brainstorming ideas for the design of your backyard and garden. Make an effort to ensure that the lines and style of your yard are consistent with those of your house. After all, the yard is only an extension of the house itself. The use of themes can assist you in determining where to place plants, decorations, hardscapes, and structures, as well as how to select those elements.

Do you want your yard to have a lot of different buildings and shapes that are clean and geometric? Do you want lines in your space to be softer and more natural? Do you want a landscape to contain only a specific range of colors? The answers to these questions will guide you toward selecting a concept for your garden. Finding Ideas for a Design Theme is the article you should read to learn more about finding ideas for your design theme. On Gardening Solutions, you will also find articles that discuss the many various kinds of gardens.

4. Create voids and link them together.4. Make spaces and connect them

Think of your yard as another room or room in your house to get the most out of it. Like a home has well-defined and carefully planned rooms, so should your landscape. Using your materials wisely allows you to make different "rooms" in your landscape. Remember to plan how your spaces will connect. How will people get from one part of your yard to another? Make openings in your yard to get people to explore and keep them moving around the landscape.

5. Use your plants to your advantage

At the start of the process, you should determine how the plants you intend to use will function in your landscape. There are a variety of applications for plants. They can provide aesthetically pleasing sights, pleasantly aromatic air, deliciously fresh fruits and veggies, and much more. You may divide up your yard into sections by using plants as dividers, and they can also serve as a marker for the edge of your property. You can construct barriers in your yard out of plants, obstructing your views and entry to a specific region. If you want to maintain some level of privacy while still having some degree of seclusion, you can utilize low-growing plants to create implied barriers that prevent entry but do not obstruct the view.

Altering the conditions of your landscape's location can also be accomplished by strategically placing plants. The temperature, the amount of light, and the wind are all significantly impacted by the trees and plants in a landscape. You can alter the sounds that are produced by your landscape by incorporating elements such as birdhouses or water features, as well as by erecting physical barriers that prevent noises from the surrounding environment from entering your garden.

6. Plan out your plants

When choosing plants, it is essential to consider their appearance from several viewpoints. To begin, you should think about the region directly above you and the plane directly above you. This may include items like arches and trees. As we go on to the vertical plane, you need to give some consideration to how far or close apart your plants will be, how they will be layered or staggered (often, larger plants go behind smaller ones), and how tall and wide they will be both individually and as a group. Keep an eye on the airplane parked on the tarmac so you can catch your flight (including how smaller plants will be grouped and arranged and groundcovers and hardscapes). Repeating the same fundamental shapes and structures over the space may give the impression that your garden is just one enormous room.

7. Point out the most important things

You can draw attention to a specific part of your landscape by using unique plants, structures, or garden ornaments. Shapes, textures, sizes, and colors that are different from each other will help draw attention to a particular area.

8. Focus on the details

The appearance of plants, hardscapes, and garden decorations varies because each component has a unique shape, color palette, and surface texture. Y By considering how these visual aspects can complement and contrast one another, you may construct a landscape that flows well and is visually attractive. Don't only concentrate on the way that your landscape will appear. The aromas produced by the plants you select for your garden can also affect how people feel while there. Consider when the flowers will blossom, how they will smell, and what other odors will work well together in the landscape. Also, consider when the flowers will bloom.

9. Think about what's to come.

To be more particular, you should think about how the passage of time will impact the plants that are a part of the landscape. When selecting plants, it is essential to consider how quickly they will mature, how much attention they require, and how big they will become. Ensure that your plants have sufficient room to reach their total potential growth. However, keep in mind that the mature size of a plant is typically determined by the optimal growing conditions under which it was grown. It all depends on the variables in your environment to determine whether a plant will expand or contract.

10. Protect your resources

You can help preserve your environment by choosing plants that use less water and other resources and hardscapes that are good for the environment. Before you take plants out of your landscaping, you should consider whether they need to go or if they could be moved to another part of your yard. When choosing new plants, look for ones that use less water, fertilizer, and pesticide and don't need as much space.

Including a rainwater collecting system in redesigning your outdoor space is something to consider. This will provide you with an environmentally friendly source of water that can be used for irrigation purposes. One could make a system like this one appear attractive as part of a design if one carefully planned it. Utilizing non-toxic preservatives, stains, paints, and cleaners, in addition to environmentally friendly hardscapes, is yet another method for defending the natural resources you own. Also, consider repurposing the materials that were used to construct the building. Before you begin ripping things down, consider what you might be able to recycle, repurpose, or include in the new landscaping design you have in mind.

TOOLS & TECHNIQUES

A thoughtfully created garden can be the pinnacle of your house, a tranquil haven where you and your family can enjoy the outdoor areas that your property offers. Similarly, many aspiring landscapers want to start working on the ideal design for their garden as garden design and landscaping continue to grow in popularity. However, it can be challenging to know where to begin if you've never designed a garden before.

This manual explains all you need to know to get started in the field of home landscaping, from design concepts to the equipment & methods you'll require:

- Landscaping for homes is an individualized activity.
- Ideas for Garden Landscape Designs

Your method for creating a lovely and serene garden will depend on several elements, such as:

- Your taste in fashion
- The garden's objectives
- Your garden's size and scope
- Your residence

Here is a list of popular garden design layouts, together with information on each one's benefits and optimal uses, to assist you in designing and organizing your garden.

Residential Urban Landscaping

A well-designed garden can act as a private haven to unwind and rest in city life's fast-paced and social atmosphere. When residing in a city, you'll probably want to create a garden that:

- Maximizes the little available space;
- Provides a break from the commotion of city life

Here are a few examples of typical city plans to get you started:

Ideal for an enclosed balcony

Paving with a long aspect is employed in this arrangement to give the appearance of more space and depth. In addition, the flowerbeds exude an aura of the enclosure, which makes them an excellent location for hosting get-togethers and relaxing. This layout is perfect for homeowners who want a stylish and social garden because it offers a large amount of space for hosting guests while also preserving the homeowner's privacy from the surrounding neighbors.

Terraced Sandstone Architecture

Raised portions are used in this layout with a woodsy theme to give it a sense of depth. A sandstone patio and surrounding vegetation are excellent for fostering a serene mood. This design is a perfect fit for those who want to construct a tranquil retreat away from the city. While it works as a balcony garden for an apartment, it is most suitable for people living in terraced homes.

Design of a Countryside Garden

Country living and landscape design go hand in hand. Whether you live in a modest country home or a sprawling rural estate, you'll undoubtedly want to enjoy the breathtaking beauty surrounding you. Here are two typical garden design concepts for those who live in rural areas:

Current ceramic design

This expansive, modern design uses wood furnishings and ceramic-copper flooring to give a rustic garden layout. The garden serves as the ideal gathering place for visitors thanks to the inverted flowerbeds that divide it into various sections.

Classic Modak Layout

A curved flower bed and hedgerow give this cozy patio area a traditional and enclosed feel. The brick accent and wooden planters merge with the orange-to-pink Modak paving, emphasizing the vibrantly colored flower garden. This design is perfect for people who live in tiny country homes or cottages since it provides a secure retreat for leisure time.

Basic Garden Design & Landscaping Tools

It's time to arm yourself with the landscaping necessities once you've chosen the plan for your garden. Here are our top four suggested landscaping equipment for homes, along with tips on what to look for when buying each one:

Gloves

The most important yet sometimes underutilized item for residential landscaping is a sturdy pair of gardening gloves. Without a set of high-quality gloves, you expose your hands to the risk of damage and nasty fungal infections. Choosing a pair of gardening gloves should take into account the following:

- Durable
- Water-resistant
- Well-fitted

Secateurs

Secateurs, sometimes referred to as pruning shears, are ideal for daily plant maintenance. High-quality secateurs will have sharp, well-angled blades to ensure a clean cut on fragile flowers, twigs, and branches. When selecting a pair of secateurs, make sure that they:

- Easily fit in your hand
- Include a sharp, high-quality blade.
- Include a catch that works well and isn't stuck.

The Bahco PX ERGO Secateurs are ideal for pruning because they come in three different sizes, have a high-quality blade, and have a smooth catch.

Hand Trowels

When you're in the trenches, hand trowels will be the foundation of your landscaping project. They are excellent all-purpose tools for weeding, planting, and transplanting. These essential criteria should be considered when selecting a set of hand trowels:

- Are stainless steel-based.
- Include a variety of blades in various sizes.
- Easy to grip and fits well into the hand

The brick trowel and brick jointer are included in a complete hand trowel set like the Faithfull Soft Grip Handle Trowel Pack, which has everything you need to implement your garden plan.

Rake

Rake In a well-planned garden, debris and falling leaves are unavoidable (especially if you followed our tip on enclosing your garden with hedges or plants). The implementation of your new landscape design will probably be a messy process as well. A high-quality rake can quickly clear away trash, leaving your yard looking tidy and clean. Make sure a rake has the following qualities before purchasing it:

- Steel tines that can bend (which prevents the soil from being damaged)
- A relaxed, lightweight grip (which keeps the rake easy to use)
- A lightweight aluminum rake like the Bulldog Evergreen Lawn Rake should handle most gardens easily.

Techniques for Garden Landscape Design

Now that you have almost everything set up, it's time to adjust your layout and begin carrying out your plans. Here are our top four methods for creating garden landscapes:

Be sure to enclose your garden.

Your garden should act as an oasis, a lovely retreat where you can enjoy the outdoors peacefully on your property.

A garden enclosure gives you a sense of isolation from the outer world, so you can unwind and enjoy it without being disturbed.

Your garden can be enclosed in one of three ways.

Fencing: The most typical method of fencing off a garden. Consider purchasing fencing with a movable screen so you may freely "open" and "shut" the outside world as you see fit.

Walling: This is a fantastic alternative if you want to give the enclosure of your garden a cozier vibe. Consider choosing more traditional walling, like the Bradstone Old Town Walling, or more modern, like the Stonemarket Avant-Garde Walling.

Plants and hedges: The alls and plants are lovely if you want the enclosure to feel more natural. In addition to being ideal for garden enclosures, shrubs also give the yard festive air.

Make the most of "borrowed" scenery.

It's wise to note any nearby landmarks or scenic vistas before fencing in your garden. The final thing you want to do is wall off or fence your garden if it overlooks a stunning view (such as a large lake or a hilltop).

Similarly, it's essential to plan the color palette and arrangement of your garden to include any notable landmarks around your home (such as churches, statues, or old buildings).

- Make Your Flower Beds Curve
- Natural growth is rarely linear.

PIdeallystraight flower beds might occasionally give your landscape a stocky, "manufactured" appearance. By using curved flower beds, you may give your garden a more natural feel and let the various areas melt into one another. Additionally, people commonly prefer curved shapes to angular ones, which makes your garden much more aesthetically pleasing.

Implement "The Golden Rectangle"

Residential landscaping methods like the golden rectangle have been used for millennia. The younger sibling of the golden ratio is this mathematical ratio (which the Ancient Egyptians used to build the great pyramids). In architecture and design, it's employed to create a sense of harmony and order. The length of your garden should be multiplied by 0.618 to structure it using the golden rectangle technique. Your short sides should be that certain number long. There you have it, then! A comprehensive manual for designing garden landscapes. Why not check through our garden design ideas if you want additional details on how, to begin with residential landscaping?

GARDENS AND STONES

When beginning a landscaping project, most gardeners naturally and automatically think about plants. However, using rocks and stones in your landscaping as stand-alone pieces or in conjunction with plants and trees can be a novel approach to adding texture, color, and interest to your yard. The terms stone and rock are frequently used interchangeably among gardeners. However, they refer to very distinct materials. On the other hand, rock is freshly separated from a more significant mass underneath the earth's surface, generally by blasting out at a quarry. In theory, a stone has been exposed to weather or water near the earth's surface for a long time.

Because the weathered stone has many rounded or fragile edges and cracks, it will function best if you're working in an area where moss can grow, such as in a moist, shady location. The lacy lichen will grow on stone but not on the cut or shattered rock-polished surfaces. Learn how to construct and maintain retaining walls using rocks and stones.

A typical starting point is to gather stones they genuinely like and use them as accents in beds or containers that attract attention. Constructing stacked stone walls is also fun; no concrete is required if the wall is less than 18 inches high. A new planting area with excellent drainage is naturally created behind the wall, and the wall itself serves as a lovely backdrop for vines and cascading flowers. Some varieties of stone can be used as practical, environmentally friendly pavers for paths. Still, careful site preparation is necessary to prevent the stones from shifting while people walk on them. Stones are required to establish a natural environment and exaggerate the water if you have a water feature. Look at some suggestions for stacked stone walls. Create a DIY water feature on your own. There are countless options; the most precious stones come from old stone cabins and fences. A terrific idea for a rock garden, typically planted with alpine plants, thymes, and other plants that require excellent drainage, is to mimic a stone "ruin" or collapsed building. Learn how to create rock gardens.

Stone may be a powerful and valuable feature in any environment since it can have a strong unifying effect on the landscape year-round. Consider how you want the area to look in two to three years, keeping in mind that the stone will dominate the scene in the winter. The goal is to produce sets where it's impossible to determine whether the stone or the garden originated first. The stone should appear and feel as though it had just been dug up; all you had to do was select the best pieces and arrange them properly, just as people have been doing for countless generations. An attractive selection of movable landscaping stones should be kept on hand by gardeners at all times. For instance, erect a stone border around a flowerbed when it is fully bloomed. Small stone pillars on the east side of the gardens can operate as early-morning basking areas for butterflies.

For big residential landscaping projects, selecting a single type of stone and sticking with it rather than varying the colors and textures is typically preferable. After all, your home, deck, and other features already have textures. A single dominating stone texture add-on looks natural, but multiple ones are unappealing. Visit stone yards to check what is reasonably priced, easily accessible, and matches any stones or boulders already existing in your yard before deciding. Find a stone that has two somewhat flat edges and is accessible as a "facing" stone. Natural breaks into facing pieces make limestone, sandstone, and other sedimentary-type rocks—formed at the bottom of lakes and seas—easy and enjoyable to work with in landscaping projects. Stone walkways and walls need to be adjusted slightly to prevent shifting caused by freezing and thawing in damp areas. Typically, I use a teapot to saturate cracks in stone walkways with boiling water to weed them out. In contrast, groups of strategically placed stones in a fern garden require no maintenance, and rock gardens frequently require less weeding than lush garden beds.

The Advantages of Rock Landscaping

Using rocks will enhance your landscaping and produce aesthetically pleasing, long-lasting results. Some unusual features that can be added to a lawn or garden using stones are walls, water features, and rock gardens. They can also serve as a durable mulch replacement that doesn't need to be changed yearly. Consider the mood they'll set for the rest of the property while selecting rocks for your landscape. White marble chips help to brighten shaded locations, while tan beach pebbles or river rocks offer warmth. While flat terracotta stones look great in a tropical setting, they may need to fit in with a more formal garden. Black lava rocks are ideal for a modern minimalist landscape or a garden with a Polynesian theme.

THE FUNCTIONS OF GARDENS

Green" landscaping your garden makes it look better, which is good for your home and the environment. This kind of landscaping can be good for your budget, health, future, and the environment. Gardening goes beyond just a hobby or something fun to do. Gardening has been shown to help people in many ways. If you spend time outside working in the dirt and caring for your plants, gardening can benefit you whether you are a hobbyist or professional horticulture. Green landscaping includes organic compost, native plants, and eco-friendly materials that will protect the environment, reduce adverse effects on the earth, and provide other environmental benefits. Here are some reasons why having a green landscape is good:

Less work to do

For green landscaping, you should choose plants that grow naturally. Native plants in your area can quickly adapt to their environment, making it easier for you to care for them. You should take care of your lawn and landscaping on the weekends, but with this type of landscaping, you can do it quickly.

Fewer Pesticides

You will use fewer pesticides if you choose plants native to your area and resistant to pests. And because of this, we can help keep the air and soil from getting dirty.

Long-Term Savings

Traditional landscaping costs 90% more than green landscaping, so green landscaping saves you money. A "rain garden" or making your yard into a natural slope could also help conserve water and protect against flooding.

Conservation

The Department of Energy says that if you put three shade trees in the right place, you can save $100–$250 on your energy bills each year. With careful planning when making a landscape, like putting shade-giving trees on the sunny sides, you can save the average amount of money on energy costs.

The functions of a garden

You are much more like your plants than you think, and your body can do photosynthesis just as well as theirs. This is where the light from the sun makes food for your plants. In the same way, your skin absorbs vitamin D in the same way when you garden. Researchers say that the sun can make between 8,000 and 50,000 international units of this vitamin, depending on the color of your skin and how much you cover it with clothes. Vitamin D helps strengthen your bones and boosts your immune system. It can also lower your risk of multiple sclerosis, non-lymphoma, Hodgkin's prostate cancer, bladder cancer, breast cancer, and colorectal cancer.

Did you know gardening may lift your disposition and make you feel more positive about yourself? You may experience a reduction in feelings of anxiety and depression if you go outside and tend to your garden. Over a few years, this benefit of gardening was investigated in one particular study. People who had been diagnosed with depression took part in a 12-week gardening program. Before and after the intervention, the researchers looked at the people's depression symptoms and other aspects of their mental health. They found that each person's symptoms improved after taking part. They also tracked the people for a few months afterward and found that the changes had lasted.

It makes you more robust in the garden.

Another good thing about gardening is that it can help you feel less stressed. It can help you heal and get back on your feet after something stressful. People were put in a stressful situation. Then they split up the group and asked one to garden and the other to read quietly. The researchers then checked how many stress hormones everyone had in their bodies. They found that the people who gardened had fewer stress hormones than those who read quietly. The gardening people also said their moods were better than those in the other group.

When you garden, you do small tasks like cutting the grass or raking that count as light or moderate exercise. But you can get moderate exercise by digging, shoveling, and chopping wood. All these things will ensure you use your muscles, which can help you get stronger. You'll use all your major muscle groups when working in your garden for a while. This is one of the best things about gardening for older people. Researchers have found that gardening can help people sleep up to seven hours a night and keep them from being overweight as they age.

Gardening can help people get over their addictions and depression.

Horticulture therapy is not a new idea that gardeners have known for a long time. Working with plants is a part of many programs that help people overcome their addictions. People trying to get over an addiction can feel good emotions and feelings from plants, making them a good tool for rehabilitation. In one study, people in a rehab program were given a chance to take part in a natural way of getting better. They could choose either gardening or art as their therapy and the people who decided gardening were more likely to finish the program and were happier.

Regular gardeners have a lower risk of cardiovascular events such as heart attacks or strokes. This is one of the most beautiful parts of gardening. You might grab your gardening equipment, get outside, and spend a few hours taking care of your plants to lessen the levels of worry and tension in your body. This could help lower your blood pressure. This puts less stress on your heart and lungs, which is a significant benefit. Persons over the age of 60 whom garden have a 30 percent lower chance of having a stroke or heart attack than those in the same age group who don't garden. This is a comparison to people in the same age group who don't garden. Investigators uncovered these results through their investigation.

Gardening Can Help You Eat Better

Because of the exorbitant cost of fresh food outside of its harvesting season, many people prefer to eat veggies that have been canned for long-term storage instead of fresh produce. Even beginner gardeners can bring in a reasonable crop of products is one of the numerous perks that come along with gardening. This is one reason why people enjoy engaging in gardening. It is feasible to save for later using a sizeable quantity of vegetables that require minimal work to cultivate earlier in the year. This can be done by preserving the vegetables in cold storage. You might even sample vegetables you have never had before, and the food you buy will be free of any herbicides or pesticides used in food processing. If you reside in a location with the right weather conditions, you can cultivate your natural fresh fruits and vegetables.

Gardening help improves mental health.

When you have challenges or a lot going on in your life, it is not uncommon for your self-esteem to take a hit as a direct result. If this is your first time working in a garden and you have no idea how proficient you'll become, this is crucial to bear in mind. One of the numerous advantages of gardening is that it can give an individual an immediate and natural boost to their sense of personal worth. This is only one of the many advantages of gardening. After you have tended to your garden by planting the seeds, watering it, pulling the weeds, and adding fertilizer, you may relax and watch it grow. The expansion of other plants will contribute to a more positive sense of self-identity on your part. Gardens offer many options to increase their knowledge and skill set, which is always enjoyable because it allows one to learn new things.

One of the numerous benefits of gardening is the increase in one's sense of success and overall happiness due to watching one's plants thrive. As your plants mature and you begin collecting their fruits and veggies, you will have a much more positive opinion of yourself and a much more favorable perception of your talents. People often remark that gardening is a moderate exercise, which is true if you have a more extensive garden with crops growing yearly. If you have a more extensive garden with crops that grow yearly, you can expect to burn more calories while gardening. If you have a more extensive garden with produce that expands annually, gardening is a sort of exercise with a level of effort that falls between light and moderate.

Gardening can make your bones stronger.

Your bones have the potential to become significantly more brittle and thin as you get older. Your body will start to produce less vitamin D, the primary vitamin that contributes to maintaining strong bones and teeth. When you work in your garden and spend time outside in the sun, your body will produce more vitamin D because of the sun's rays. Every time you step outside while dressed in shorts and T-shirts, you can take in the maximum amount of physical vitamin D possible. This vitamin D can prevent your bones from becoming fragile and brittle. People with high blood pressure are more exposed to experiencing cardiovascular problems. One of the many advantages of gardening is that it can help lower blood pressure naturally, eliminating medication in some cases. One way to accomplish this is by reducing the levels of anxiety and tension you experience as a direct result of the amount of time spent tending to your plants. People with indoor gardens or plants go through a similar experience, given that all living things require care. Your heart health will directly improve to the amount of time and attention you devote to caring for them when your blood pressure goes down—the amount of work your arteries have to accomplish also decreases.

Gardening can help with long-term pain.

Many people have joint pain that lasts for a long time. They can get stiff, which makes it painful to move them, so people don't. This makes the pain worse, so they don't carry them. Some of the stiffness caused by long-term pain could be eased by gardening. You could start small and work daily to care for a Mediterranean herb garden in your home. Planting, watering, and taking care of the herbs will help you move your joints, which can help ease some of the pain you feel. If your chronic pain is caused by arthritis, moving around can help you move more and reduce swelling. Getting tired is a nice side effect of being outside for a few hours. It also eliminates any anxious or stressful thoughts that keep you up at night, which can help you fall asleep quickly. You can also get a moderate workout by pulling weeds and taking care of your garden, making you feel more tired. Then, you should be able to fall asleep faster, sleep better, and feel ready to face the day when you wake up. If you garden every day, you might sleep better at night.

If you garden, you save money.

Gardening may help you save money, whether you focus on growing fruit trees or vegetables. You may start your garden for little money by purchasing seeds, and you can use fertilizer to make the food left over in the kitchen. Both of these things can be done in your kitchen. Collecting and storing rainwater as an additional resource for watering your plants is also possible. Even a modest garden can produce a significant amount of vegetables, which, if properly preserved, can be enjoyed throughout the entire year. Because of this, you won't need to put aside money specifically for purchasing fruits, veggies, or herbs, which will save you money at the grocery store. If you can harvest your food in the fall and winter, you will be better positioned to save money during these more expensive times. If you can use them, you don't have to worry about worrying about when you can eat organic fruits, veggies, and herbs.

Gardening can help people be more creative.

One of the most attractive things about gardening is that it gives you room to develop your creative side, which is fitting considering that gardening is all about being creative. You are free to use your imagination while planning the layout of your vegetable garden to make the most of the available area or determining which veggies would thrive in the company of others. If you have children, you can help them be more creative by asking them to help you set up and take care of the garden. They can even make cute garden signs to help you keep track of where you planted and which vegetables. Everyone learns new skills at the same time, which is a bonus. Mindfulness is a state of paying attention to the present moment. This is often seen when people meditate. You can get the same feeling by gardening, however. One good thing about gardening is that you can put all of your attention on the task at hand. This could mean getting rid of all the weeds, planting everything in the right spot, or keeping an eye on your vegetables so you can pick them up at the best time.

You can get lost in what you're doing and spend hours ensuring everything is healthy in your garden. When gardening, especially if you have a more extensive garden, you must remember much information. This benefit of gardening makes your mind sharper and helps you remember things better simultaneously. Studies have shown that gardening lets you track more than one thing at once. You need to remember where you planted each vegetable, what it needs, if you used your natural fertilizer, how often to water it, and when it's best to pick your vegetables. You use more of your brain, which can help you think more clearly.

Gardening lets you spend time with your family.

Maintaining a healthy relationship with one's family is of the utmost importance, but doing so in this day and age can be challenging. A significant amount of time is spent by many families in front of screens, but gardening can will help you limit the time spent on the task. You can use the bonding potential of gardening to get closer to your children by involving them in the enjoyment. Please allow them to select garden areas they would like to tend to and assist them in doing so. Teach them everything needed to know about growing their food, and when the time comes, allow them to assist you in storing or preparing the food they have grown. This might help you spend quality time together throughout the year. By devoting a portion of each week's schedule to the upkeep of the family garden, you will have the opportunity to catch up with each household member and learn about the activities they have been participating in. Additionally, this opportunity is open to anyone of any age and level of expertise.

Everyone in the family may learn responsibility in a way that is both enjoyable and uncomplicated by participating in a family garden, which is one of the many advantages of gardening. Your kids will see what happens if they let weeds take over their garden and if they don't water it right. You can make each part of the garden fit the needs of each child or family member. Please give them the job of helping you keep it healthy and picking your fruits and vegetables when it comes. This can also make people want to spend time outside and do things with their families. Gardening can help you feel like you have a purpose in life. It's a way to care for and grow something from a tiny seed to a big plant. When the plants start to grow, this is sometimes enough to give you a sense of purpose and pride. Whether taking on a big project like growing raspberries or a small one like caring for a houseplant, you'll feel the same way. You can keep this sense of purpose going by growing plants all year.

LANDSCAPE STEPS

After you have completed an accurate inventory of your belongings, you may move on to making a wish list of additional items you would like to acquire. How do you envision the appearance of your garden? First, jot down a few broad goals you want to accomplish. Take, for example:

• Do you want a patio to be quiet?
• Is curb appeal or resale value more important to you than a more private (patio) display?
• Do you want to block a view you don't like?

If you already have flower beds, take note of the plants doing well and fill in the gaps with the colors, heights, foliage, and bloom times you need to get the look you want. When you go shopping, this will assist you in locating the appropriate plants. If you know that your garden will have few colors after July 4, you might choose plants that bloom later instead of buying other plants that bloom in the spring if you realize that your garden will have few colors after that date. Be sure to maximize the potential of the resources you already possess. Refrain from attempting to cultivate veggies in an arid and rocky area. Instead, please use it to create a rock garden with sedums, hens, and chicks, both of which thrive in conditions that are difficult to cultivate.

Use containers to call people's attention to areas that require it. Altering them to reflect the changing of the seasons is an option if you want to make the best of the opportunity to demonstrate your talent for design on a more intimate scale. Have a look all around your neighborhood. Plants can take a wide variety of forms, dimensions, and hues. What gardens do you like? Which characteristics of plants, such as their colors, shapes, textures, and sizes, make you feel a certain way?

Pick Your Garden Look

The style and fashion of your home should match the style of your garden. Gardening is like decorating the inside of your home, but instead of fabrics, paint, and furniture, you will use the color, texture, shape, size, and placement of plants to set a mood.

- Informal: This style is a middle ground between formal and natural. It has a lot of curves and colors, lush growth, asymmetry, and trees and shrubs that look like they grew that way. The atmosphere is cozy and calm.
- Formal: This style is characterized by straight lines, symmetry, beautiful focal points like statues and fountains, well-kept lawns, and trimmed hedges. The structure is more important than the color, and the mood is refined and calm.

Natural: This style looks like nature, is easy to take care of, and should fit in with its surroundings, which could be anything from a meadow of wildflowers to a bog. The mood can be chaotic and out of control or full of life and energy.

Figuring out what you need

You'll need places for your young children or grandchildren to play if you have them. Same for pets. Look for "bulletproof" plants that can handle being stepped on, like low-growing sedum or ground phlox. Look at your front door. Do you want a front garden that makes people feel welcome and leads them to your door? Use straight paths and lines to show people where you want them to go.

Keep a small garden space from putting you on. Small plots can look bigger by lining up paths, gates, and trees to make sight lines that let the view flow from one area to the next. Also, think about how many small groups of different colored flowers can make a space look crowded, while groups of flowers with similar colors and textures can make a small space feel more open.

Make your place to get away. Use more giant shrubs and ornamental grasses to make a place to rest and relax, like this bench in the middle of nowhere. Here, you can focus on the garden and enjoy what you've grown.

Hardscape before planting

It might be tempting to start with the plants, but it's better to take care of the hardscape first. Once that is done, you can begin planting, which is fun—plant trees or shrubs as your first step. Start with the house and move out. Plan for how big the trees and shrubs will get so you don't have to move them when they get too big for their space. When you put deciduous shrubs in front of evergreens, the look will change with the seasons. Don't forget to choose some shrubs that will look good in the winter, like witch hazel or forsythia.

Use a hose or rope to make plans for flowerbeds. Fewer, smoother curves look more natural than a lot of sharp ones. Most borders are planted next to a wall, fence, or hedge and can only be seen from one side. Beds are harder to hide because they can be seen from every angle. To tend to the plants in wide beds and borders without trampling anything or compacting the soil, you need a rigid walkway or stepping stones to walk on.

Define where your flower garden ends and the lawn begins. A physical barrier made of metal, vinyl, granite, or brick will help keep grass from growing into the beds. The look can be gentler by letting plants in the foreground grow over this edge.

Stack plants based on how tall they are. To give the garden rhythm, repeat groups of plants that look the same. When you look at a garden from far away, it's best to see large blocks of the same plant rather than a bunch of different plants in one area. Consider the size, shape, leaf color and texture, flower color, and visual weight of the plants you want to put together. Loose and open or heavy and dense?

Plants with big leaves like hostas go well with small, delicate leaves like astilbe. Even when they don't have flowers, plants with blue-green, chartreuse, bronze, burgundy, and silver leaves add color to the garden. Remember that warm colors seem to move forward, and cool colors seem to move back. White can separate colors that don't go well together and bring light to a dark spot.

With a realistic and well-thought-out plan for landscaping, you can spread the work and costs out over a few years. Take things steadily so that your project becomes manageable. Remember that this is meant to be fun! You are making a place where you can enjoy yourself. Small, steady changes over time can turn your yard into the paradise you've always wanted.

DECORATIVE ELEMENTS

The line is one of the most practical and essential elements in the design process. The garden is riddled with bars at every turn. Consider the base of a tree, the horizon in the far distance, or the boundary between a lawn and the adjacent woods. A driveway, a sidewalk, or a fence are examples of distinct lines in the landscape that are simple to locate. Keep in mind the lines created by the elements you add to your garden as you plan and design it. There are primarily four ways in which lines can be described: curved, straight, horizontal, or vertical. Because each has unique effects, none can be considered more significant. Strong lines can lead people's gaze into the landscape and direct their movement through the environment.

Paths and freeform garden beds are made more interesting with curved lines. The use of straight lines conveys the appearance of a more formal sense of order and crispness. Curved lines add interest to paths and freeform garden beds. Straight lines give off a more formal feeling of order and crispness. Horizontal lines are calming and give a sense of stability. Think about the ocean and how its wide surface meets the sky. This creates a sense of peace and grandeur that can't be denied. Vertical lines give the impression that something is intense and moving.

No matter what kind of lines you use, keep in mind that they lead the eye. Lines on the ground that go away from you pull you forward. Lines on the floor make you move more slowly. Lines that go up and out of the garden draw the eye. The eye is taken on an exciting journey by lines that curve. All are desirable. It would help to determine where the lines or your sight will take you and what you will see when you arrive.

Light

What could be more breathtaking than being in the garden in the young hours of the morning or the later hours of the evening, when the plants are illuminated by a warm backlight and appear glowing? Nothing, that's what. Who could argue that plants do not require light to survive? The amount of light and shadow that color is exposed to affects how it appears and interacts with other colors. You have no control over natural light, but you can use it to your advantage. Warm colors and bright sunshine have the same effect, making an object or region appear as though it were physically closer than it is. Remember that light can come from the sun or a machine. Adding a low-voltage lighting system is simple so that you can enjoy your garden even after dark. The placement has different effects on different fixtures. A particular feature stands out when a dark area is lit from the front. Backlighting makes a sculpture, tree, or bush look like a silhouette. Sidelighting, which can also be used to create dramatic effects, is mainly used to make walkways and paths safer.

Texture

Mix plants with fine, medium, and rough textures to create balance and a little drama. Texture evokes emotional responses. Textures that are both visible and felt make you want to touch them. Use texture to make groups of plants stand out or to hide the lines of buildings. Plants can be divided into three groups based on their texture: coarse, medium, and refined. Plants, hardscaping materials, or garden structures with a rough texture have large or strongly textured parts, like rhubarb leaves or an arbor made from rough-cut 8x8 posts. Many ferns and grasses have fine textures, as do delicate structures like a bent-wire trellis or arbor. Textures that are in the middle are medium.

Texture

Texture changes can be small, and the textures of different plants (and other things) are relative. When you look at ornamental grass, it might look like a plant with thin leaves. But if you compare it to zoysiagrass, which has a much finer texture, it might look coarser. You'll find smooth, rough, rippled, and frilly textures and countless ways to combine them to create repetition, contrast, balance, and unity. All of these things are in a good garden. Plants' leaves are often what makes them interesting to touch. Plants with small leaves make dots, while grasses, irises, and daylilies make lovely, smooth stripes. A classic combination is smooth hostas with astilbe's feathery flowers and jagged leaves.

Form

Trees and bushes can look different. A good home landscape has big plants with at least two or three different shapes. A landscape without solid and diverse forms is just as hard to understand as a song without a beat. Plants and other things in the garden can divide space, close off areas, and add architectural interest. Putting plants together shows off their shapes and creates different effects. Round shapes, like those of boxwood or barberry shrubs, give a mixed border shape and stability. A series makes a rhythm of rounded shapes that move back and forth.

Stability

Stability is also added by narrow verticals that are repeated. Tall arborvitae or skinny cacti looks strange on their own. They look good when they are grouped. Strong fence posts give a sense of security and completion.

Scale

Scale, also known as proportion, refers to the relative size of one thing concerning another. A tree that is 30 feet tall would look out of place in the middle of a little patio, but a dwarf tree would fit in perfectly. On the other hand, a large mansion dwarfs the front walk, which is only a few feet wide and lined with flower strips. Before you plant a tree, consider how large it will eventually become. If it grows so large that it looms over the front of the home, even the most stunning tree in the world will appear odd and out of place. It might look lovely around the house if that tree was in the rear yard instead of the front yard.

Pattern

A pattern is created when shapes are repeated in a predetermined manner. Designs lend things a charming and rhythmic quality. It contributes additional texture and a distinct difference. It would help to consider light and shadow as part of the palette when designing patterns. Make use of ways to call attention to a particular area, but avoid using excessive bold patterns, as this can be overwhelming. Apply this guideline while you're designing the backdrops as well. You might, for instance, install bricks in a herringbone pattern on your pathways, patios, entryways, and driveway borders to bring cohesion to your hardscape. Use marks to point people in the right direction as they navigate the garden.

Balance

The picture looks balanced when the things on each side of a natural or made-up axis are the same. If you focus too much energy on one side of the garden, your eye will be drawn there instead of the garden as a whole. Balance comes in two primary forms: symmetrical (formal) and asymmetrical (informal). To find balance, you need to find a point in the middle from which to draw an axis. It could be a tree in the backyard, the front door, or something else. Balance that is symmetrical or formal is easiest to see and understand: The things on either side of a natural or made-up line are exact copies of each other. This kind of balance can be seen in the pool garden below.

Balance only sometimes fits the style of a home or garden. You may like informal balance, also called "asymmetrical balance." For example, three smaller trees on the right can balance out a large tree on the left. Or, a small group of hot colors on one side can be balanced by a large group of cool colors on the other.

Unity

This is called unity, when all of the basic rules of garden design come together to make a balanced, harmonious whole. Focusing on harmony will help you choose from a wide range of plants and other landscaping materials that can be exciting and sometimes confusing. Make simplicity a goal as well, and you'll likely end up with a design that looks and feels like it fits together. The perfect place for your favorite trees, shrubs, groundcovers, flowers, and seasonal containers is where the overall design has a good structure and the hardscape meets your needs for service and enjoyment.

Contrast

Contrast draws attention to how different something is from its surroundings. Using difference is the best way to keep a garden from becoming dull. It also makes the other parts feel more enjoyable. As with most garden design ideas, a little contrast is good, but too much can make the eye feel confused and tense. You can contrast by playing with form, texture, and color, among other things. For example, you can create a unique look by planting the different shapes of horizontal 'Bar Harbor' juniper in front of red-twigged dogwood. You can use dithered scaping materials, like bricks and gravel, or other plant textures, like a magnolia with leathery leaves next to a cedar or juniper shrub with fine needles. Lastly, the different colors of flower petals can make for great contrasts. For the colors to work best, they should be far apart on the color wheel. For example, the most different colors are red and green, purple and orange, and yellow and blue. You can also put green and purple leaves next to leaves with various patterns.

Color

Color draws the eye, makes you feel confident, and changes with the seasons. Color works in predictable ways as a powerful and unifying tool. Cool colors like blues, purples, and greens calm and move away, while warm colors like reds, oranges, and yellows energize and move forward. The simplicity of one-color schemes is what makes them so appealing. Putting colors together to show off your personality is where the real fun is. Some colors fight for attention, while others work well together. Even though flowers are the garden's jewels, too many different colors make the garden look messy. Remember that a balance makes a pleasing effect of only slightly different colors.

Rhythm

You can create rhythm and repetition when you place or contrast things correctly. The rhythm keeps things from getting boring. Even though a garden may be complete in almost every way, it might only seem attractive once it has a rhythm, like a line of shade trees along a drive or the same pattern of pavers or pickets in a fence. These parts make it clear that something is moving.

Only some literal repeats are needed for rhythm. It can be done with the help of a line. The path shown here curves similarly but in different ways. Also, the vertical lines of the bamboo help create a sense of rhythm by repeatedly being used in the same routine. The gradual change along a planting bed from warm colors and rough textures to more excellent colors and finer textures and back to warm and uneven textures are other examples of rhythm. As different plants bloom and then die back so that others can take their place, there will still be a pleasing visual rhythm.

WILD LANDSCAPES

Wild landscapes are a popular decoration, but what are they exactly? Many people feel wildness is a part of nature far away from their everyday lives. And yet, we are constantly surrounded by the situations and species that make character alive and change. Wild nature is trying to get in through the cracks of our modern lives. Wolves and mountain lions, important predators, can sometimes be found in cities. Native bees can often find better places to eat in empty lots. Birds and butterflies fly through our yards but don't stay long.

Adding wildness doesn't mean having a space that isn't clean or that you like ticks. It means we must rethink how we relate to nature and how to make a healthy home through a more thoughtful way of designing gardens. Wildlife needs wild places. Studies have shown that bees find more flowers in run-down urban areas and well-designed suburban backyards than in row-cropped fields, where flowers are only found in thin strips along the field edges. But we don't have to have what some people call a "weedy landscape." This space has many different colors, shapes, and textures that still need to be taken care of.

We can plant a wild garden in a way that still has some order. This can mean using plants that are native to the area and that native animals need to live their lives. It can mean planting grasses and flowers in big clumps along sidewalks or parks, or putting coneflowers, poppy mallow, or asters in city planters. Wildness in the city can mean using less fertilizer and pesticides. Wildness can be as easy as letting a milkweed plant that blew in on the wind grow next to a straight line of lilies.

Wildness to save energy.

By placing plants around our buildings in an intelligent way, we can save money on cooling and heating costs and help stop climate change. Shrubs along a house's south and west walls and a mix of tall and short trees in the understory can reduce the amount of sun that hits home while also making essential habitats for wildlife. Even vines growing on a trellis against a wall can help keep a building cool. Conifers in the north can slow the winter winds and give songbirds a place to hide. Landscapes that let water collect or soak in slowly after it rains help us use fewer resources to make clean water for our gardens. When we use plants suited to their environment, from the sun to the soil, we can almost eliminate the need for fertilizers, which take a lot of water and energy.

Healing in the wild

At first, it can be scary to walk through the woods, wade in the ocean, or get lost on a trail in the desert. Our bodies get tense and alert when we leave the comfort of what we know. Once we overcome our fear of dark forests and waves that roll in and out, something constantly changes inside us. We calm down, let go of our preconceptions, and find our place in a rhythm that pulses through everything that lives. We can hear this rhythm in how the switchgrass in our backyard sounds like the switchgrass in the prairie or the fountain bubbles like a mountain stream.

There's a reason why butterfly gardens are popping up outside hospitals and treatment centers and why street trees add much value to neighborhoods and homes. We know in our bones that being in nature makes us feel better and more interested in caring for our towns and each other.

Treebeard

We can go somewhere else to find wild places. It's what we do. We need every part of nature to be healthy, connected, and hopeful. When we make gardens that are good for us and other species, we remember how privileged we are to be alive and how important it is to pass on our good fortune to the next generation.

APPLYING LANDSCAPE TO THE HOME GARDEN

Landscape design principles are rules used to make landscapes look nice. Using landscape design principles, you can make a place that is both comfortable and nice. These things are beneficial when changing a flower garden, a shade garden, or a new garden space.

Using the rules of landscape design

Order is a term for the way the landscape is set up. This idea is also called "Balance" because a good balance is a way to keep things in order. Ratio means giving weight and visual appeal equal value by using different colors, shapes, textures, and sizes. You create balance by repeating similar parts where it makes sense. Designers create symmetrical balance by putting similar things on opposite sides of an axis. On opposite sides of a garden, they can put plants, trees, or flowers that look alike. This method seems reasonable because the items are spread out evenly, and there is symmetry.

This landscape design idea can also be used with asymmetrical balance. Landscapers make an asymmetrical balance by giving different shapes, colors, or textures the same amount of visual weight. This can be done by putting groups of trees or garden decorations on each side of the axis that looks the same but has different qualities. Perspective balance means that the foreground, middle ground, and background look the same. Designers give the illusion of depth by putting bigger things or brighter colors in the background to balance the bigger things in the foreground.

Proportion

Landscapers must ensure that the sizes of the plants, decorations, and structures they use are all the same and fit a person's height. The size of the plants must be suitable for the average person, house, or plants around them. In the same way, there should be as much open space as there is space with plants. Designers can create dominance by putting together big and small plants or create harmony by putting together plants of the same size.

The hardscape should be both functional and appealing to look at. Using the tables, benches, gazebos, and paths should be easy and comfortable. Designers should also balance open spaces by closing off small areas. You can use this landscape design idea on a patio or other site.

Unity

Landscapers create unity by linking design elements or features to create a theme that runs through the whole piece. They can use different methods, like dominance or connection, to create harmony and a character that makes sense. The best way to ensure everything fits together is to start with a design style or theme in mind and plan the landscape around it. By making a particular shape, plant, or object the focal point of the landscape, unity by dominance is achieved. The thing stands out because it's different from what's around it. It could be a flowering plant with unusual features or a group of brightly colored flowers meant to attract hummingbirds or butterflies.

Creating unity through interconnection means making links between parts that fit together. Hardscapes are often used to connect different landscape parts because they link other places together. With fences, stairs, walkways, and paths, you can physically connect different areas with this landscape design idea.

Repetition

Repetition is when design elements or features are used more than once to make a pattern or sequence. Designers can make repetition by using the same line, color, texture, or shape over and over again. You can make repetition more interesting by using alternation, in which a slight change in the order of things makes a new pattern.

Inversion is a type of repetition in which the next thing in the sequence is the opposite of the one that came before it. For example, you could use this landscape design element by putting cone-shaped shrubs next to canopies. Gradations are shapes where the main feature changes slowly over time, like when the size of a circle gets smaller and smaller over time. Instead of patterns, repetition can also be seen in the same shapes or colors across the landscape. Landscapers must be careful with repetition because too much of it can get boring.

Conclusion

Your yard is an essential natural resource that increases the value of your home and makes your life more enjoyable. It helps make the community a nice and healthy place to live. Several important ideas will help you make a design that looks good, works well, and lasts for a long time. First, remember to write down your thoughts: make a plan. Use the design process to determine your site and what you need.

Use a theme to help you decide what to do. Professional designers always look at the space to get ideas for materials and plants. A key concept in design is to make spaces that can be used as outdoor rooms. For functionality and psychological comfort, areas that are the right size for people are best. Use plant material for the walls, ceilings, and floors of the rooms to create a microclimate that is good for your health. If you consider that plants evolve through time, you'll discover that observing the transformations can be a satisfying aspect of maintaining a garden. The only remaining areas of green space in many of our cities are private backyards. Consider how your garden fits into the bigger picture and what you can do to improve the environment in your community.

www.ingramcontent.com/pod-product-compliance
Lightning Source LLC
Chambersburg PA
CBHW081627100526
44590CB00021B/3631